LAKE DISTRICT
A RARE INSIGHT

SIMON REED

First published 2018

Destinworld Publishing Ltd
3 Fairfax Road
Middleton St George
Darlington, Co. Durham DL2 1HF
www.destinworld.com

British Library Cataloguing in Publication Data.
A catalogue record for this book is available from the British Library.

Printed and bound in Bulgaria by pulsioprint.co.uk

ISBN 978-0-9955307-8-2

CONTENTS

ENGLISH LAKE DISTRICT

Bothel
Caldbeck
Hesket-New-Market
Uldale
Overwater
Embleton Golf Course
Castle Inn
Greystoke
Penrith
Cockermouth
Piel Wyke
Bassenthwaite Lake
Mungrisdale
Skiddaw
Saddleback
Lorton
Troutbeck
Whinlatter Pass
Keswick
Threlkeld
Dalemain Park
Pooley Bridge
Loweswater
Braithwaite
Lowther Castle
Scalehill
Derwentwater
Dockray
Ullswater
Crummock Water
Aira Force
Howtown
Buttermere
Lodore
Glenridding
Bampton
Buttermere
Grange
Thirlmere
Patterdale
Shap
Borrowdale
Honister Pass
Rosthwaite
Helvellyn
Hawes Water
Ennerdale Water
Seatoller
Dunmail Raise
Brothers Water
Mardale
Great Gable
Styhead Pass
Langdale Pikes
Kirkstone Pass
Wastdale Head
Scafell Pike
Grasmere
Grasmere Lake
Rydal Water
Gosforth
Scafell
Ambleside
Kentmere
Wastwater
Elter Water
Wastdale
Boot
Hard Knott Pass
Windermere
Drigg
Eskdale Green
Coniston
Hawkshead
Bowness
Ravenglass
Coniston Old Man
Torver
Esthwaite Water
Ulpha
Coniston Water
Windermere Lake
Kendal
Oxenholme
Bootle
Broughton
Lake Side
Whitbeck
Newby Bridge
Silecroft
Greenodd
Milnthorpe
Millom
Ulverston
Cartmel
Dalton
Grange-over-Sands
Furness Abbey
Carnforth
Barrow
MORECAMBE
WALNEY I.
BAY
Bolton-le-Sands
Morecambe
Scale in miles
0 ½ 1 2 3 4 5 6 7 8 9 10

BLACKPOOL 25 MILES

The English Lake District covers an area within the county of Cumbria, with twelve main lakes and many of the country's highest peaks.

INTRODUCTION

People from all over the world come to Cumbria every year to marvel at the beauty of the Lake District, which is arguably one of the most scenic regions of the United Kingdom. The landscape is ancient, and history is everywhere in the buildings and ways of life of the people who live here. Yet the region has also adapted, with modern amenities and businesses catering for the tourists and locals of the region. With this in mind I set about collating the record of life in the Lake District and how its valleys, villages and people used to look over the past hundred years or so. The result is this book, which I hope will attract your interest even more in this, my favourite part of the world. I hope that it will also show you how the buildings and scenes so familiar today have changed over the years, yet the charm and attraction of the region has only grown.

The region known as the Lake District, or the Lakes, is one of the greatest rural areas of the British Isles, steeped in traditional ways of life and working the land which have been adapted to suit the sometimes inhospitable and difficult terrain.

This region, which today is in the county of Cumbria, features many great mountains and hills, and England's highest peak at Scafell Pike. The valleys below these peaks are home to many rural communities, farms and even uninhabited places completely off the beaten track.

Then there are the lakes for which the region takes its name – all 19 of the major bodies of water, alongside many smaller tarns. Whilst providing a scenic backdrop and a means of leisure activities, these lakes were mostly formed following the last ice age, with a few man-made reservoirs added into the mix. They include Windermere, which is the largest natural lake in England, and Wast Water, which is the deepest.

The Lake District was one of the first areas in the country to be designated a National Park in 1951. This set to protect the area and its natural beauty from over development, preserving it for the enjoyment of the people who had already started flocking here by the 18th century.

Indeed, it is also the largest of the National Parks, and was extended in 2016. In 2017 a further accolade was bestowed upon the Lake District when it was designated a UNESCO World Heritage Site owing to its beauty, agriculture and the inspiration it has proved to artists and writers – none more famous than William Wordsworth, John Ruskin, W G Collingwood and Beatrix Potter. These and many others have found homes and meaning in their works through spending time in this region.

Those with a love of the outdoors have always been drawn to the Lake District because of its peaks and valleys. Every peak above 3,000ft in England is within the Lake District, and miles upon miles of paths and walkways have been established over them and around them. Many come to try climbing every "Wainwright" peak (so-named by Arthur Wainwright who published guides to walking them), and choose to stay at one of the remote huts provided for walkers, or perhaps while away evenings in a traditional pub in one of the villages scattered throughout the valleys.

The pictures that follow are separated into the northern and southern sections of the Lake District National Park, with a separate chapter on the areas around Windermere, which is one of the most visited tourist centres and areas for outdoor activities.

Crummock Water — Bassenthwaite Lake — Buttermere — Rydal Water — Windermere — Ullswater — Wast Water — Thirlmere — Coniston Water — Grasmere — Derwent Water — Esthwaite Water

TWELVE LAKES

C1771

AROUND WINDERMERE

"THE SWIFT" ON WINDERMERE.

Windermere is the largest natural lake in England measuring 10.5 miles in length and one mile in width. The lake has always been busy with commercial traffic generated by the copper, slate, wool and fish industries and in the 19th century there was a fleet of boats that took passengers and goods to and from Ambleside, Bowness, Hawkshead and Newby Bridge. From Newby Bridge there were stage coaches to Lancaster and the Whitehaven stagecoach stopped at Ambleside. The first steamboat on Windermere was *The Lady of the Lake* which was launched in 1845. Since then, there have been many steamers in service on the lake including the *Dragonfly, Firefly* and *Swan*.

Windermere is a hive of activity in this early painted scene, with rowing boats and sailboats crowding the shores.

The Neo-Gothic towers of Wray Castle form an impressive backdrop to this romantic scene looking across Lake Windermere from the shores near Ecclerigg, with boats and wildlife on the waters. Wray Castle was actually built in 1840, and is therefore much younger than the view would have you believe.

Bowness on Windermere (the Ordnance Survey gave it this name to avoid confusion with other places in Cumbria with the same name) has always been intrinsically linked with boats. Originally it was a boat building community making yachts, rowing boats and steamers. Today visitors can enjoy a lake cruise and there is a regular passenger and car ferry service.

368. Windermere and Bowness, from Biskey Howe.

Biskey Howe is a twisting road high above the centre of Bowness. It provides the perfect view across Windermere, and is still a popular place to take in the scene today.

F.W. Hayes

Waterhead,
Windermere.

The artist of this scene may have taken some liberties in defining the dramatic rises of the hills above Windermere, but nevertheless Waterhead, near Ambleside, is a lovely place to view the lake. Whilst tourist developments and homes have crept upon the water's edge somewhat today, the lake is still popular for boating.

Bowness lies in the useful position at the narrowest point of Lake Windermere. Because of this, a ferry service across the lake has existed for a long time. In this picture a motor car from the early 1900s seems to almost be causing the ferry to lean to one side. The passengers are looking back at the camera with interest.

A horse and cart and many people dressed in elegant Edwardian clothing occupy the Promenade at Bowness where it fronts Windermere. In the background a lake steamer emits a plume of smoke into the sky. Today this is a busy road, yet it is still a place full of visitors moving between the town and the boats.

A lovely view looking north up Lake Windermere from the western shore at Mitchell Wyke Bay, where the ferry traverses the lake's narrowest point. The Ferry Hotel mentioned in the postcard's caption is now a private residence alongside the pier.

Skelwith Force is a really pretty 16ft (4.8 metres) waterfall on the banks of the Brathay not far from Ambleside and is can be seen on the popular walk from Skelwith to Elterwater

Lakeside is the small town at the southern tip of Lake Windermere. It has a railway station and is linked to the lake's steamer ferry services, giving it easy access to tourists. To the left of this view, Windermere empties into the River Leven and ultimately Morecambe Bay a few miles to the south.

Several miles west from Grange-over-Sands is Newby Bridge with its lovely five-arched bridge (built in 1651) that spans the River Leven. Newby Bridge has a lovely old station for the preserved Lakeside and Haverthwaite Railway.

Troutbeck is an old village that is strung out along the main road from Windermere to Penrith. At the beginning of the village there is a series of drinking troughs. These were for horses making the long and arduous journey through Kirkstone. The parish church is dedicated to Jesus and was built in the 18th century. A peep inside reveals some beautiful stained-glass windows.

Waterhead at the northern end of Lake Windermere seen at a much more tranquil time in its recent history. Today this same view would be crowded during the busy tourist season.

All manner of waterborne craft are visible in this scene looking over the harbour and piers at Bowness-on-Windermere, including the classic lake steamer coming in to dock.

The Belsay Hotel, from which this picture was taken, is now a boutique hotel operated by Laura Ashley, still with the same magnificent views over the lake.

The Macdonald Old England Hotel is one of the finest four-star hotels in the Lake District, offering its guests stunning panoramic views of Lake Windermere with the chance to enjoy fine dining, the hotel spa and private jetty. It has been around for many years, with an unrivalled position near Bowness.

Another view of the Old England Hotel on the shore at Bowness-on-Windermere. This time the camera is positioned further out to reveal the lake steamer Swift crammed full of passengers ready to travel up and down the lake.

There are a variety of boats and vessels that can be enjoyed on Windermere and lake cruises on them vary in length between 40 minutes – three hours.

The proximity of Bowness to the lake, and the comings and goings of the lake steamers and other craft, have always drawn crowds of visitors to the shoreline. In this 1940s view the steamer has just departed for Lakeside.

A wonderful scene of rural life in the Lake District which is so different to today. Children and their mother, or perhaps a teacher, stand in the lane posing for the camera whilst others walk off towards the village of Near Sawrey.

A gothic boathouse in a secluded bay on Lake Windermere is the perfect companion to the scene of Wray Castle towering on its hillside position above. Beatrix Potter once spent a holiday at the castle before she relocated to the Lake District, however she never owned the castle. Today it is a National Trust property.

Compared to some of the other featured scenes of Bowness Bay, this painted view is much quieter without the crowds of ferry passengers along the piers. This scene also looks south towards Windermere's narrowest point.

E589. HEAD OF WINDERMERE FROM BEDROOM BALCONY
ROMNEY HOTEL, WATERHEAD, AMBLESIDE.

Some lucky guests would be greeted by this view from the Romney Hotel at Waterhead every morning. Just visible is a lake cruiser pulling in to the pier, and the view of Windermere stretching beyond.

The Swan steamer approaching Lakeside Pier which is situated at the southern end of Windermere. Passengers can get on the steamer and travel either to Waterhead or Bowness.

As well as being the place to catch one of the steamers, Lakeside Pier is the end of the Lakeland and Haverthwaite Railway with its marvellous steam trains. It is possible to climb onboard and travel to Haverthwaite enjoying the sheer nostalgia evoked by steam.

The magnificent St Mary's Church in Ambleside was designed by prolific Gothic-style architect George Gilbert Scott in the 1850s, and has to be one of the most scenic in the Lake District at the heart of Ambleside.

A long-lost institution in Waterhead, near Ambleside, was the Romney Hotel. Its position next to the head of Lake Windermere is evident here, with a magnificent view from its rooms. It was demolished in the 1980s.

Stock Beck runs through the heart of Ambleside, tumbling over this weir among the centuries old houses and mills. Many of these building survive, yet the overriding industry of the town today is tourism.

Looking along the shore at Waterhead near Ambleside. Lake Windermere reaches its northernmost point here, with reeds growing from the shallow waters.

The crowded lake steamer Tern leaves the pier at Bowness, sailing north to Waterhead Bay near Ambleside. The lake steamers on Windermere were developed by the Furness Railway as an extension of their service into Lakeside at the southern end of Windermere. MV Tern was built in 1891.

H 41/214   THE HOUSE ON THE BRIDGE,   AMBLESIDE.

Bridge House in central Ambleside was built in the 17th century and survives to this day, attracting thousands of tourists every year. It was built by a family who wanted access to their lands on either side of Stock Beck, which runs underneath the quirky house.

Ambleside seen from above, looking down from the path leading up Loughrigg to the east of the town. The summit of Loughrigg Fell offers magnificent views in all directions.

By the Lake at Bowness-on-Windermere.

For centuries Bowness was a small fishing and boat building community on the shores of Lake Windermere in the Southern Lakes. Its name comes from the Old English words *bulner* (bull) and *naess* (headland} a reference to the fact that bulls grazed in the vicinity. The arrival of the railway in the 19th century turned Bowness into a popular holiday destination – which did not please the local poet William Wordsworth who wanted the Lakes to remain quiet and unspoilt. Today, most of the town's residents are involved in the tourist trade.

Those who have read Arthur Ransome's *Swallows & Amazons* will recognise that Bowness is the Lakeland town of '*Rio*' in the books.

THE NORTHERN LAKES

The Jaws of Borrowdale   358

The incredible glaciated landscape of the Borrowdale valley has long fascinated visitors. Where the valley narrows and the towering heights of Kings How and Castle Crag rise above the road and rushing river, the valley has earned the name 'The Jaws of Borrowdale'. Its teeth are the summit of Castle Crag which is visible in the centre of this image.

The treacherous routes through the fells and mountainous areas of the Lake District are amply demonstrated in this coloured postcard showing coaches negotiating a bend known as 'The Devil's Elbow'. The caption helpfully places this view as being on the route between Buttermere and Keswick, with the likeliest location being near present day Keskadale Farm in the Newlands Pass.

780. "A Cattle Scene." Derwentwater and Lodore. Keswick.

Even the local livestock are known to enjoy the beauty of the Lake District. As these cows paddle, the view is drawn south across Derwentwater towards Borrowdale and Lodore, near the village of Grange.

99 GRANGE, BORROWDALE (ABRAHAMS SERIES)

Grange is the first village south of Derwentwater and about four miles from Keswick. It is a small, pretty village and reached by the twin-arched bridge. It is well known for its good climbs which include Little Chamonix, Shepherd's Crag and the Gillercombe Pinnacle.

The Bowder Stone, Borrowdale   153

Arguably one of the Lake District's most famous sights is the 2,000-ton Bowder Stone, which measures 50ft across and 30ft high. As if to demonstrate its size, the lady posing underneath in this photograph is dwarfed and almost hidden. The staircase allows a great view from the summit.

BRAITHWAITE, 416.

Situated in the northern lakes, at the eastern end of the Whinlatter Pass and Forest is the village of Braithwaite. It is popular for all kinds of sports including walking, rambling, sailing, canoeing, hang gliding and bird watching as there are many species of birds to be spotted in the area including ospreys.

Mellbreak is a mountain which dominates this area, covering almost the entire western side of Crummock Water. With a summit standing 1,680ft above sea level, it sits in isolation which gives it greater prominence among the surroundings.

The southern tip of Crummock Water, where two small islands sit just of the shore. Another side of Mellbreak rises out of the misty low cloud in the centre of the picture, framing the old sail boats nicely. Crummock Water is a much quieter lake compared to Derwentwater, Ullswater and Windermere.

Looking from its head, Ullswater is indeed a fine ribbon lake – a classic example of glaciation. It is the second largest of the lakes. By the 1890s, Ullswater had become a fashionable holiday destination because it offered good sailing and shooting on the surrounding estates.

Castlerigg is situated on the eastern side of Keswick and dates from 3000BC. When excavations were carried out on the land within the stone circle a number of Neolithic tools and farming implements were uncovered.

A quiet view of Howtown Bay in a secluded corner along the southern shore of Ullswater. The landing pier is visible, but few other signs of life can be seen. The location is still quiet and tranquil today.

Nestling on the eastern banks of Thirlmere is the delightful little Whythburne Church with its white-washed walls and green slate roof. There has been a church on this site since the 15th century and Coleridge once described it as 'a humble house of prayer.' That it may be but its location with Helvellyn as a backdrop is stunning.

The old bridges across St John's Beck to the north of Thirlmere. This whole area changed dramatically in the 19th century when Thirlmere was chosen to become a dam that would serve the Manchester area. The existing lake grew significantly, flooding much of the surrounding agricultural land.

Prior to the construction of the dam across Thirlmere, it was possible to cross the lake over a bridge at its central point, as seen here in this rare old view looking south along the much smaller, original lake. The bridge was often swept away during floods, and is now completely swamped by the modern reservoir.

Seatoller, Borrowdale   143

Here the Honister Pass descends into the Borrowdale Valley, where you'll find the lovely village of Seatoller at the heart of the Lakes. Little has changed with this scene today, other than the introduction of the modern motor car and a few more visitors. A National Trust car park at the village acts as a base for exploring the area.

794 Rosthwaite Valley and Church.

Rosthwaite Valley to the south of Keswick and Derwentwater. In this photograph from the hillside, the flat glaciated valley can clearly be seen, along with traditional farmsteads and church before the roads became busy with motor vehicles.

The tiny hamlet of Watendlath offers some of the best views of the dramatic Derwent Valley. For fishermen there is the added delight of being able to relax and enjoy their surroundings whilst casting a line into the natural seven-acre Watendlath Tarn.

Mists over Scawdel Fell, Grange - in - Borrowdale 325

Separating the Newlands and Borrowdale valleys is a mountain which many walkers and climbers know today as High Spy, but which was commonly known in the past as Scawdel Fell. The mists in this view add to the sense of drama and inaccessible heights of the peak, which is over 2,100ft above sea level.

Keswick Lake, as described here, is actually Derwentwater. The series of piers along Lake Road are still a popular place to catch a launch or take a rowing boat onto the water, or even across to Derwent Isle where the 18th century house is open to visitors. The summit of Skiddaw makes a dramatic backdrop.

The church of the Holy Trinity at Seathwaite sits in the Duddon Valley. It was built in 1871 on the site of a much older church. The curate there served for 69 years and the poet William Wordsworth described him as 'a wonderful walker'.

4006 Aira Force, Ullswater

Aira Force at Ullswater is the most visited waterfall in the Lakes. It dramatically tumbles 65ft (19.8 metres) and perfectly captures all that William Wordsworth loved about the Lakes.

The area was developed by the Howards of Greystoke Castle into landscaped gardens to appeal to Victorian visitors. More than half a million trees and shrubs were planted and in 1846 an arboretum was developed with more than 200 species of conifers from all over the world. There are two simple stone bridges at Aira Force – one is dramatically at the start of the falls - and these were built by a Watermillock family as memorials for family members.

Round about Patterdale.

Close to Glendidding at the end of Ullswater is Patterdale – a popular place with climbers as one of the routes up Helvellyn begins just outside the village. Although not many visitors have time to explore Patterdale, it is worth popping in the village church which has some lovely tapestries. Here schoolchildren are seen outside the village school.

Hartsop in Patterdale is at the start of the Kirkstone Pass. Among its historic buildings is the 17th century Old Spinning Gallery with its balcony where spinning of yarn could continue under cover during bad weather, without losing the natural light. A number of houses in the area featured such a gallery.

The famous Moot Hall that stands in the centre of Main Street in Keswick has been used for a variety of things over the year. The first building to stand on the spot was built in 1571 at a time when Keswick was the centre of the copper mining and a place was needed that could be 'used to weigh, mark and coin the copper'. The current building, seen here, dates from 1813 and old records show that a market used to be held on the ground floor each week. Over the years, the Moot Hall has been used as a courthouse, prison, museum and as the Town Hall. Today the Moot Hall is used as a Tourist Information Centre. The clock on its western end is very distinctive as it only has one hand.

The medieval Long Bridge crossing the River Derwent at Portinscale carried the coach road from Kendal to Cockermouth. Its unusual twin-arch span was much admired by locals, who were in uproar at the proposal of it being demolished. However, nature would have the final say when floods damaged the bridge beyond repair in 1954. A pedestrian bridge spans the gap today.

75. KESWICK AND DERWENTWATER.

The market town of Keswick lies just ten minutes' walk north from Derwentwater. It is a beautiful lake with the fells (including Cat Bells) to its west, the well-known vantage point of Friar's Crag jutting in to the lake on its eastern side, and Borrowdale to its south. There is much to see and enjoy in the area including an open-air theatre on the shores of the lake by the town.

CROSTHWAITE CHURCH, KESWICK.

The medieval church of St Kentigern on the outskirts of Keswick, known as Crosthwaite Parish Church. One of its previous vicars was Hardwicke Rawnsley, who was a co-founder of the National Trust in 1895. He is buried in the churchyard here, along with the poet Robert Southey.

Fitz Park is situated just minutes from the centre of Keswick and is great fun for all ages. It has been enjoyed for decades, as seen in this postcard from the early 1900s. The lower park has a children's play area as well as a large area for playing with balls – and during the summer months the local cricket team can be seen in action there. The upper part of Fitz Park is a formal landscaped garden with numerous specimens of different shrubs and trees

The Keswick Hotel (now known as The Keswick Country House Hotel) stands close to Fitz Park and is an elegant Victorian building built in 1869. Its location is popular with guests as both the town centre and the shores of Derwentwater are just a few minutes' walk away.

County Corner and Penrith Road in the centre of Keswick with early motor cars lining the quiet streets. The war memorial seen on the corner opposite the camera was unveiled in 1922.

WORDSWORTHS HOUSE. COCKERMOUTH.   Copyright.

Sitting just outside the limits of the National Park, Cockermouth was the home of William Wordsworth as a child in the 1770s. His Georgian townhouse home seen here is today a museum to the writer, showcasing his work and the environment in which he was born. Many original artefacts are on display.

Grange - in - Borrowdale. View from Peace Howe   172

Peace Howe near Grange-in-Borrowdale is a war memorial looking out over the flat valley that shows the classic signs of glaciation – and if you need more evidence, the nearby Bowder Stone is said to have been carried by the glaciers from Scotland and now sits about a mile from Grange.

LODORE FALLS, KESWICK.

Tumbling over 100ft through oak woodlands into the Borrowdale valley and ultimately Derwentwater are the legendary Lodore Falls, one of the most attractive waterfalls in the Lake District.

Robert Southey so loved the falls that he penned the poem on the following page in their honour. Today, visitors can reach the waterfall from the Lodore Falls Hotel.

Lodore Falls in Summer.

"How does the water come down at Lodore ?"
A dry-season Tourist once thought to explore,
But he failed to discover the famous cascade,
So enquired in despair of a Cumbrian maid ;
"Indeed, Sir," quoth she, with a toss of her bonnet,
Ye may well seek Lodore, for ye're sitting upon it ! "

Many would argue that Derwentwater is one of the most beautiful lakes, especially when the water looks like a mirror reflecting the sky and Skiddaw rises as a magnificent backdrop. The River Derwent rises high in Borrowdale which lies to the south of the lake, with Keswick at the other end of the lake. Derwentwater is sizeable as it measures three miles in length and one mile in width. There are four islands on the lake: Lord (once home to the Earl of Derwent), Derwent, St Herbert's and Rampsholme and three smaller islets: Park Neb, Otter and Otterbield.

An early view of the Derwentwater Hotel, set in its own grounds close to Keswick and Derwentwater at Portinscale.

703 HEATHERY HEIGHTS
ABOVE DERWENTWATER
VIEW FROM WALLA CRAG
(ABRAHAM'S SERIES)

Walla Crag overlooking Calfclose Bay and Derwentwater stands at an easy-to-remember 1,234ft above sea level. For those who don't want to scale its summit, it looks just as impressive when seen from the lake.

Armathwaite Hotel is an impressive looking 17th century building that was once a stately home. The hotel is situated in 400 acres of deer park and woodland overlooking Bassenthwaite near Keswick. The hotel offers guests spectacular views of Skiddaw.

Greta Hall in Keswick is one of the most important monuments to the Lakes' poets, for both Samuel Taylor Coleridge and Robert Southey lived here at different times in the early 1800s. Many of their friends and contemporaries visited the house during this time, including Lord Byron, William Wordsworth, John Keats, Percy Shelley, Sir Walter Scott and John Ruskin. Following a period as a girls' school, it is now a bed and breakfast accommodation.

Friars Crag is a headland that juts out into Derwentwater just close to the boat landings. It is said that it was given its name as it was the point where monks used to cross on pilgrimage to St Herbert's Island to its southwest.

721. FRIARS' CRAG AND GRISEDALE PIKE.
DERWENTWATER. KESWICK.

Grisedale Pike lies west of Keswick and is distinctive as it has its main summit at 2,593ft (791 metres) and two lower secondary summits. Most walkers take the route from Braithwaite up the eastern ridge. The views from the summit are good. Keswick and Derwentwater as well as Blencathra and the Vale of Keswick can all be seen clearly as can the lofty summit of Skiddaw.

The mythical 'floating island' which can appear during the summer on Derwentwater, created by masses of vegetation appearing on the surface on rising methane gas.

A motor launch comes in to dock at the pier near Keswick with a fine view of the Cat Bells fell on the western side of Derwentwater.

Howtown is the name given to a small hamlet, bay and harbour on the eastern shores of Ullswater, about three miles (5km) from Pooley Bridge. Howtown is said to mean *'farmstead on the hill'* but interestingly it is the surname of the family that lived in the farmstead and it was they who built the Howtown Hotel too. Situated in Howtown Bay is a popular outdoor education centre for those who would love to learn how best to enjoy the Lakes.

Glenridding is situated at the southern end of Ullswater and its name means 'overgrown with brambles'! It developed as a community in the 17th century when iron ore was discovered there, and Greenside Lead Mine opened. The mine closed in the 1960s as it was unprofitable, and tourism became the village's main source of income.

For the energetic, Glenridding is the start of the popular climb up to Striding Edge near the summit of Helvellyn, whilst those seeking relaxation can take the 19th century lake steamers *Lady of the Lake* or *Raven* and explore the lake's 8.5 miles of beauty, travelling to Pooley Bridge at the other end or making the journey in reverse.

Bassenthwaite is the most northerly lake and is impressively long and narrow, measuring four miles in length but less than a mile in width. Interestingly, there are no sizeable communities on its shores. Like Derwentwater, it is home to the rare species of freshwater fish known as Vendace whose numbers declined sharply in the 1960s and can now only be found in these two locations.

The Whinlatter Pass cuts through Thornthwaite Forest linking the village of Braithwaite at one end with the twin communities of High and Low Lorton at the other. At the top of the pass is an interesting Visitors' Centre which reveals the rich history and wildlife of the area.

This isolated lake is one of the most beautiful of all in the Lake District and it is perfect for those seeking solitude. Haweswater is actually a reservoir that was created on the site of an old village and it is said that the remnants of the old buildings can be seen in the water. The reservoir is fed by a stream and there is a walk around its shores which takes just under five hours to complete.

"Solitude" Crummock Water 871

Many postcards showing Crummock Water included the title "Solitude". In fact, Alfred Wainwright said in his 'Pictorial Guide to the Lakeland Fells': "it is the view across the lake, where the water laps the sterile base of Mellbreak far beneath the mountain's dark escarpment, where loneliness, solitude and silence prevail that make the scene unforgettable."

452 Pooley Bridge. Ullswater

At the other end of Ullswater, by the River Eamont is the village of Pooley Bridge. The village was given its name from the large pool in the river close by. It had a pretty 16th century bridge that crossed the river until recent floods caused its demise. The river flows on to Langwathby where it joins the River Eden.

Near Seathwaite the character of Borrowdale changes dramatically as a small side valley joins the main river valley and the road and river are forced through a narrow gorge known as the 'Jaws of Borrowdale'. The other side of the gorge is very different again as the land stretches out into wide open pastures.

St Patrick's Well can be found just one mile from Glenridding (2.2km). The well dates from AD 450 when St Patrick, Patron Saint of Ireland, is said to have preached on the shores of Ullswater. He baptised local people using water from the well and since then people have believed in the holiness of the water which is said to cure people who are sick. Interestingly, as late as the 15th century, the dale was also called *Patrick's Dale* but over the years the name changed into *Patterdale*.

Watendlath is the name of both a hamlet and a tarn near Grange, near Keswick. The tarn is seven acres in size and its waters flow into the beck of the same name and then into the Lodore Falls where the water tumbles over huge boulders for a distance of about 100ft until the water finds its way into Derwentwater.

Although the pier is for getting on and off the steamer, many enthusiastic photographers have discovered that it is perfect for capturing glorious sunsets, the passing seasons and changing moods of the beautiful lake. If you would like to climb aboard a steamer, there is a selection of different routes across length and breadth of the lake with journey times from 20-120 minutes.

Spring is a beautiful time in Ullswater and a walk along the lake in 1804, with his sister, Dorothy, inspired Wordsworth to write the best-known poem in the English language...
I wandered lonely as a cloud
That floats on high o'er Vales and Hills,
When all at once I saw a crowd
A host of dancing daffodils;
Along the Lake, beneath the trees,
Ten thousand dancing in the breeze.

Another scene of the dramatic mountainscape rising above Crummock Water, also featuring the 'Solitude' title. Note the lack of evidence of human life or any boating activity, which makes this lake one of the most tranquil to visit.

9795 BRIDGE BY VICTORIA HOTEL BUTTERMERE — JUDGES LTD

The Bridge Inn was built upon the site of an old armoury in the village of Buttermere, between the lake of the same name and its northern neighbour Crummock Water. Its name was changed to the Victoria Inn in 1850 when the queen visited. Today the name has reverted to the Bridge Hotel. The B5289 still passes over this quaint bridge.

The Raven at Pooley Bridge, Ullswater   S.644

There have been steamers on Ullswater for more than 170 years and they offer passengers stunning views of popular fells including Helvellyn. The steamers can be boarded at Pooley Bridge, Howtown and Glenridding at the other end of the lake and certain steamers stop at the National Trust pier at Aira Force.

Rosthwaite Valley and Skiddaw, 3176.

Rosthwaite is a small community in Borrowdale, to the south of Derwentwater. Rosthwaite lies six miles (9.7 km) from Keswick and once again, is popular with walkers as there is a particularly good walk to Watendlath. There has been a community there for centuries as it was first a Norse settlement and given the name 'Rosthwaite' meaning *'a pile of stones'*

In 1900 a memorial to John Ruskin was unveiled above Friar's Crag, as seen here. John Ruskin was the leading Victorian art critic and water colourist who had many ties with Keswick and thought Keswick was almost too beautiful to live in.

THIRLMERE LAKE.

Thirlmere was a natural lake that was dammed at its northern end in the 19th century and turned into a reservoir to supply the growing town of Manchester with water. The water was (and still is) taken to Manchester by the 96-mile-long (154 km) Thirlmere Aqueduct.

There have been steamers on Ullswater for more than 150 years and they are 'environmentally friendly'. There are various landings on the lake and Pooley Bridge is one of its most popular both with walkers and families who enjoy tackling some of the low-level walks or playing on the lake shore beaches.

The Kail Pot is a craggy fell, just under Hallin, overlooking Ullswater. Immediately below the crags is a pool of dark, deep water that is perfect for jumping into on a hot summer's day! The perilous climb up the cliff face is demonstrated here in an age before safety equipment was common among climbers.

PEAKS AND PASSES

The usual route to ascend Striding Edge is from Patterdale and Glenridding, walking up through 'Hole in the Wall' before starting the ascent which is where the breeze definitely picks up and first-time climbers feel quite exposed. Many people who tackle Striding Edge prefer to descend via Swirral Edge – another popular scramble.

Honister Pass and Crag. There is a lovely circular drive that explores the area from Keswick through Newlands Pass and onto Crummock water Buttermere.

The life of a Cumbrian shepherd is not an easy one, especially in the gruelling winter months. They work tirelessly caring for their flocks especially at lambing times and during the outbreak of disease like foot and mouth. *The Shepherd's Life: A Tale of the Lake District* by James Rebanks gives an interesting insight into their lives.

SCAWFELL PINNACLE.   4009.

Pronounced Scawfell, the peak of Scafell Pike is a highlight of the Lake District for anyone who enjoys climbing. Here, the precarious rock formation known as Scawfell Pinnacle has been conquered by a brave climber.

Black Sail Hut in Ennerdale is a youth hostel which is famous the world over for being the most remote, as it is situated in a car-free valley and can only be reached on foot. If you really want to experience being in the Lakes, Black Sail Hut offers you total peace and isolation, countless inquisitive Herdwick and plenty of Cumbrian rain!

Sheep are a common sight in the Lakes and indeed sheep farming has long been the cornerstone of the area's economy. There are more than three million sheep in the area today.

Lying two miles from Coniston, Tarn Hows is one of the most visited beauty spots in the Lake District. It was originally three separate tarns, but these were joined together in the 18th century. Beatrix Potter loved Tarn Hows and bought it, bequeathing it to the National Trust upon her death.

The small lake lies just 1.5 miles (2.4 km) from Hawkshead is perfect for picnics in the summer and a great place to skate in the winter!

Striding Edge, Helvellyn. 209

Helvellyn is a ridge of mountains that run north to south in the Lakes between Ullswater and Thirlmere. It is Striding Edge, a razor thin ridge on its eastern shoulder, which attracts thrill seekers to climb. Striding Edge is officially a scramble and a relatively easy one at that, so with good walking boots, a map and plenty of common sense it is achievable, but best tackled in good weather.

Windy Gap is a high and, in the winter, very bleak pass that links the dome-shaped Great Gable with the smaller fell of Green Gable.

Sprinkling Tarn is a pretty tarn but not nearly as well known as Skyhead Tarn. The two can be linked in a circular walk from Seathwaite that is not too arduous but rewards walkers with good views of Great Gable and Great End. In this early picture, a walker reflects on the scenery only the Lakes can offer.

At 1,489ft (454 metres) Kirkstone Pass is the highest pass in the Lakes that is open to traffic (weather permitting). Kirkstone links Ambleside in the Rothay Valley with Patterdale in the Ullswater Valley and gets its name from a large and unusually shaped rock that stands by the roadside which many say looks like a church – or *kirk*. Over the years, lead and copper have been mined here and today there is slate mining near the summit.

Great Langdale is one of the major valleys in the Lake District with the smaller Little Langdale close by.

The Langdale Pikes are a group of peaks situated in Great Langdale that offer climbers great views and are always high on their must-climb lists. A popular circular route leaves New Dungeon Ghyll and climbs six of the tops including Pike O' Stickle (2,326ft) with has a distinctive lump of rock on its summit

Whilst horses were used for many years by shepherds as a method of transport between their herds, they would say that their most prized animal was their sheepdog. Well trained sheepdogs make driving and shedding sheep easier and work in close partnership with their master, obeying every whistle and command perfectly. Here an obedient dog walks alongside his master on horseback.

Stickle Tarn is situated in the Langdales, close to Stickle Ghyll with its hydroelectric station. The tarn is in an impressive location as it surrounded by Harrison Stickle, Pavey Ark and Pike O' Stickle which were once part of the rim of an old volcano. The tarn was enlarged and dammed in 1838 so that it could be used to supply water to Langdale.

538. A LAKELAND LANE.

There are three breeds of fell sheep that have been developed since medieval times which are particularly suited to life in the Lakes. The hardiest of the breeds is the Hardwick, and with the Swaledale they are the breeds that can be seen grazing high on the fells in the most appalling weather. Their wool is much sought after by knitters! The third breed is the Rough Fell, and it too can withstand extremes of temperature. There are three lowland breeds farmed in the lakes which can usually be seen grazing in meadows and fields in the valleys.

THE BORROWDALE VALLEY FROM GREAT END
"ROGUE HERRIES COUNTRY" 1899.

The Borrowdale Valley is situated in the central lakes and heads northwest with the vale of Keswick and Derwentwater at one end. Wainwright considered Borrowdale to be the finest square mile in the Lake District. It is also referred to as 'Rogue Herrie's country' as the character from Hugh Walpole's popular series of four books lived in the area. Hugh Walpole himself moved to Cat Bells overlooking Derwentwater for the final years of his life. The valley can be explored throughout the year as there is a good bus service along its length.

148A TOP OF CATBELL'S.

Cat Bells (1,480ft / 450 metres) is definitely one of the most popular climbs in the Lake District. Much of its popularity comes from the instantly recognisable silhouette of the mountain, and it is not such a difficult climb so can be enjoyed by all the family. Cat Bells is situated on the western shores of Derwentwater so offers climbers beautiful views over the lake. The name Cat Bells is said to have come from the Cumbrian dialect meaning *'home of the wild cat'.*

106. Buttermere and Crummock from Honister.

Close to Crummock Water lies Buttermere, which has always been popular with visitors. It is a particularly beautiful lake, seen here in the valley below, and has a circular walk around its shores. In the little church of St James there is a stone tablet on one of the windowsills remembering Alfred Wainwright who wrote the famous walking guides to the Lake District. The view through the window is of his beloved Haystacks (which is always worth the climb) like nearby Red Pike as both offer spectacular views over Buttermere.

In Neolithic times the Langdale Pikes were an important area for producing stone axes and other tools. Later, Langdale became the centre of the Lakeland slate industry.

Situated in the Southern Lakes is Scafell Pike – at 3,208ft (978 metres) the highest mountain in England. Scafell is actually part of a horseshoe of fells and from its summit there are great views of Borrowdale, Eskdale and Wasdale. Scafell is one of the 'Three Peak Challenge' with Ben Nevis in Scotland and Snowdon in Wales being the others.

Honister Pass and Crag.

Ye simple tourists, who so cheerful pay
O'er Honister Pass to drive in "four
    horse shay,"
This painful truth experience will tell,
It's mostly walk and pay your fare as
    well.

The perils of early travellers paying for passage over Honister Pass is described perfectly in this poem and illustration. Today, there is a lovely circular drive that explores the area from Keswick through Newlands Pass and onto Crummock water Buttermere.

Pillar Rock is credited as being the place where rock climbing began. In 1826 a local man climbed to its top purely for fun and within years it had become a popular sport, developing alongside tourism in the Lake District.

The remote and elevated position of Sprinkling Tarn is shown here high above the valley leading to Derwentwater, which is just visible on the right of the image.

Sprinkling Tarn has the honour of being one of the wettest places in England. It is also a popular fishing location.

3105 Honister Pass and Crag. (New Road).

Situated in the heart of the Lakes, Honister Pass is one of the highest passes in the Lake District with a gradient of 1 in 4. It begins at the southern end of Buttermere and links the Buttermere valley with the eastern end of Borrowdale. It is best known for the slate mines at its head which are great fun to visit. Westmoreland Green Slate which is 400 million years old is still mined there and visiting the site gives a great insight into the industry.

The view of Great Gable from Wasdale is one of the most popular and impressive in the Lake District. The mountain gives the impression of a mystical pyramid rising above the surroundings.

THE SOUTHERN LAKES

HHD.3.

WORDSWORTH SCHOOL. HAWKSHEAD.

Hawkshead's Grammar School, which operated on the site from 1585 until 1909, was attended by the Poet Laureate William Wordsworth. Today it is a popular museum.

Branthwaite Brow in Kendal is a lovely cobbled street that leads down to the river. It is the perfect place for wandering as it has a number of speciality shops including its famous chocolate shop and tailors' workshop. In this historic image we can see a public house along with a fish and poultry dealer.

The Parish Church of the Holy Trinity in Kendal is impressively wide as it has five aisles, and in fact it is one of the widest in England, making it one of the largest parish churches too. There has been a church on the site since Anglo Saxon times but the current building dates from the 18th century. The church is also known for its magnificent peel of ten bells.

KENDAL HOTEL, KENDAL

An early image of the Kendal Hotel and public house at the heart of one of the main towns in the southern Lakeland region. Today this building is still evident, but now used as a shop and private residences.

Kendal is a delightful market town situated in the southern lakes and for many years was one of the country's leading centres for the production of woollen cloth. There used to be workshops producing other fabrics too and a leather tannery. Today Kendal is best known for its mint cake which is produced in brown and white varieties and is perfect for sustaining energy levels for walkers!

Tiny Boot village is situated in Eskdale and is the only coastal village in the Lake District National Park. The village developed when iron was discovered in the red sandstone of one of its northern fells and Nab Gill Mine was established with a railway linking it to Ravenglass. The mine continued working until December 1912 when it was deemed unprofitable as the supply of iron had been exhausted.

In the centre of Boot Village stands a distinctive 17th century packhorse bridge over the beck. Close to the village is Stanley Ghyll Force an impressive waterfall that drops 60ft (18.3m) through a narrow gorge where beautiful rhododendrons grow.

4175.8. Hoad Hill and Sir John Barrow's Monument.

This impressive monument was built in 1850 of limestone from Birkrigg and paid for by public money. The monument itself is 100ft (30.5 metres) tall and stands on the summit of Hoad Hill, so is known locally as 'the Hoad Monument'. It reminds people of Sir John Burrow who was born in Ulverston and became Second Secretary to the Admiralty running the British Navy.

E 792/205 UPPER ESKDALE.

Eskdale stretches from the west coast of Cumbria at Gosforth, eastwards to the foot of the Hard Knott pass. It is dramatically beautiful with many classic signs of glaciation, but interestingly does not contain a lake.

2057. Grange over Sands from Grange Hotel.

Although it lies just seven miles (11 kilometres) from Windermere, Grange over Sands is completely different in character as it is a pretty coastal resort on the shores of Morecambe Bay. Grange over Sands was once a tiny fishing hamlet, but it became popular in Edwardian times and developed rapidly - its expansion aided by the development of the Furness Railway. Its estuary is rich in birdlife and popular with ornithologists.

THE HALL, HOLKER HALL.

Inside the private Holker Hall near Cartmel which originally dates from the 16th century, but was largely rebuilt in the 19th century. It is the home of Lord Cavendish, with magnificent grounds often open to the public.

Edwardian visitors enjoy a stroll along the Promenade at Grange-over-Sands, which is nestled between the main road and the town's railway station. Today, the area of water we see here has largely been reclaimed by vegetation and sand.

The Grade I listed Muncaster Castle lies a short distance inland from Ravenglass in the south-western Lake District. The present structure has origins dating back over 800 years, however it is thought a Roman fort may have been on the site prior to this.

Visitors today can enjoy the castle and its gardens, which are still a private home. Among its highlights are the pele tower and great hall.

Guests visiting Hawkshead today can stay in this Grade II listed cottage, which was once home to Ann Tyson and her husband Hugh, with whom William Wordsworth boarded during his time at the nearby grammar school in the 1780s.

An early 17th century house in Hawkshead known as the Pillar House for obvious reasons. Its first-floor juts out, supported by pillars and accessed via an external staircase. It can still be seen behind the church of St Michael and All Angels, and was common of a style of building seen throughout the village.

Another example of a house supported by pillars. Hawkshead is one of the oldest settlements still in use in the Lake District, dating back to the period of Norse occupation, and the founding of nearby Furness Abbey.

Another view of the old grammar school in Hawkshead. The east end of the village church is visible behind, along with the top of its tower.

What was perhaps once another pillared house on Main Street in Hawkshead. Parts of this building are now incorporated into the Beatrix Potter Gallery, which is a popular attraction in Hawkshead. The Red Lion Inn can be seen just beyond.

Inside Hawkshead's Grammar School which is now a museum and shows original schoolroom furniture, including desks with graffiti from William Wordsworth and his brother John.

Near the former Roman baths, known as Walls Castle, was a beacon above Ravenglass and the harbour called Newtown Knott. It could be seen from miles around, and used to help ships navigate into the harbour. Today the Knott is a tumble of ruins, but still makes for a nice walk with stunning views.

A few miles inland from Grange-over-Sands is Cartmel Priory, founded for the Augustinian Canons in 1190. The church dates largely from the 14th century, making it one of the oldest in the area, and still serves as the parish church for Cartmel.

Inside the priory's church, which is dedicated to St Mary the Virgin and St Michael. The choir screen dates from the 16th century, added following the Dissolution of the Monasteries when Cartmel survived intact.

Wastwater is an interesting lake. It lies amongst the highest fells – Scafell, Great Gable, Kirk Fell and Red Pike. It measures three miles (4.8 km) in length but is just half a mile wide. With a depth of 260ft (792 metres) it is the deepest lake in England.

Wastwater is well known for the solid banks of scree along one side, known as 'The Screes'. These rise nearly 2,000ft (609 metres) – which is fun for scree running but best avoided by general walkers.

July 27th 1908.

The beautiful red sandstone ruins of Furness Abbey lie in a valley just north of Barrow in Furness and hint at its importance and wealth as a monastery.

FURNESS ABBEY, Chapter House, Interior /826/

Built in the 12th century, Furness Abbey was actually the second wealthiest Cistercian monastery in England at its peak.

Beatrix Potter bought Hill Top in Near Sawrey (there is a Far Sawrey too) in 1905, paid for from the royalties of her first book. Four years later she also bought Castle Farm. Hill Top is traditionally built, with stone walls and a slate roof. It was here that she wrote many of her famous children's stories and where such much loved characters as Jemima Puddle Duck were created.

Beatrix Potter loved the Lake District and championed many aspects of local life, including Herdwick sheep. She died in 1945 having written 26 successful children's stories and she left 4,000 acres of land in the Lakes to the National Trust, including her beloved Hill Top – with the stipulation that it could not be changed in any way and that the furniture and china must stay just as she left it... so to this day, stepping into Hill Top is stepping back into yesterday and it is one of the most visited places in Cumbria.

High Nibthwaite is a small village in the southern Lakes that lies on the eastern side of Coniston. In the past it had both a forge and furnace but this closed in the mid-19th century. It was here that the young Arthur Ransome came on holiday with his family which later inspired him to write his five famous *Swallows & Amazons* books.

Dove Cottage was bought by the poet William Wordsworth (1790-1850) with his sister Dorothy and it is situated on the outskirts of Grasmere at Townend. The building was once an inn known as 'the Dove and Olive Bough'.

Wordsworth lived at Dove Cottage for eight years and it is where he wrote some of his greatest poetry. He married Mary Hutchinson whilst he was living there, and three of their five children were born at Dove Cottage.

Red Bank, Grasmere.

(The steepest coach-road
in Lake Land).

Red Bank was steep, descent
was rash,
Full soon there came a woeful
smash.
A link snapped in the chain:
A passing native gave a shout
Of guileless satire "Eh, come
out!
What? is ta flayt o' rain?"

Red Bank is the name of a road and area at the end of Grasmere which is particularly steep. This poem tells of the woes which often befell drivers tackling the downward slope.

Walkers, however, thoroughly enjoy the downward descent through Red Bank to the lake side where there is a good footpath to follow.

Poet's seat is situated overlooking Rydal Water – one of the smallest lakes which measures just three quarters of a mile long and a quarter mile wide. The lake was much loved by the poet William Wordsworth and the seat has been erected on the spot where he enjoyed the best views of the lake.

Many visitors to the Lake District seek out Wordsworth's grave in St Oswald's churchyard at Grasmere. However, those that venture inside the church are greeted by this timber roof, the arches and stained-glass windows, much of which dates originally from the 14th century.

Two miles south of Kendal, in the Southern Lakes, is Natland – popular with walkers as there are so many good walks to enjoy in the vicinity – including one along the old canal towpath and the other along the river Kent towards Kendal.

St Mark's Church, seen here, was opened in 1910 having been much enlarged from previous churches on the site to cope with the large congregation.

Situated in the western Lakes, Wasdale can be a remote and wild area. It is the widest Lakeland valley and in it lies Wastwater- the deepest lake- and the highest mountains of Great Gable and Scafell. It is where England's smallest church can be found – St Olaf's with its thick slate roof covering sturdy wooden trunks said to have come from Viking ships.

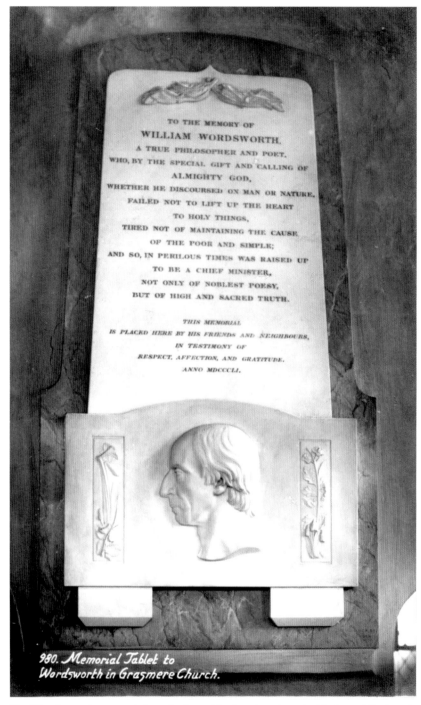

TO THE MEMORY OF
WILLIAM WORDSWORTH,
A TRUE PHILOSOPHER AND POET,
WHO, BY THE SPECIAL GIFT AND CALLING OF
ALMIGHTY GOD,
WHETHER HE DISCOURSED ON MAN OR NATURE,
FAILED NOT TO LIFT UP THE HEART
TO HOLY THINGS,
TIRED NOT OF MAINTAINING THE CAUSE
OF THE POOR AND SIMPLE;
AND SO, IN PERILOUS TIMES WAS RAISED UP
TO BE A CHIEF MINISTER,
NOT ONLY OF NOBLEST POESY,
BUT OF HIGH AND SACRED TRUTH.

THIS MEMORIAL
IS PLACED HERE BY HIS FRIENDS AND NEIGHBOURS,
IN TESTIMONY OF
RESPECT, AFFECTION, AND GRATITUDE.
ANNO MDCCCLI.

980. *Memorial Tablet to Wordsworth in Grasmere Church.*

The Wordsworth memorial can be found in the churchyard of St Oswald's church in Grasmere and is dedicated to the poet and his wife, Mary. This memorial is one of the most visited places in the Lake District.

Rydal is a small hamlet in the southern Lakes, standing close to Rydal Water and situated halfway between Grasmere and Ambleside. It is a popular place to visit as it is where William Wordsworth settled after leaving Grasmere and his home - Rydal Mount - can still be seen. It is an attractive area to visit, with a pretty church and some good walks – that the poet particularly loved.

As well as the monument inside St Oswald's church in Grasmere, in the churchyard outside is the grave of the poet and his wife Mary, who died nine years after him. Other members of his family are buried in the churchyard, in which he personally planted eight of the yew trees you can see today.

Literary fans flock to this location, which has been one of the most visited sights in the Lake District since his death in 1850.

Rydal Water.

Rydal Water is one of the smallest lakes, close to the hamlet of Rydal. It, too, has close ties to the poet Wordsworth who loved the lake and found it inspirational for many of his poems. At the western end of the lake, steps lead to the Wordsworth Memorial – offering visitors the view he particularly loved. There is a pleasant walk around the lake.

Another pretty view of William Wordsworth's former home, Rydal Mount, not far from Ambleside.

The poet was a keen landscape gardener, and this postcard from the early 1900s shows off his handiwork in front of the house.

A lovely scene of the stepping stones over the River Rothay in Rydal, a short distance from Rydal Water at the end of the village.

Pelter Bridge is a more comfortable way to cross the Rothay than the previously-shown stepping stones. The bridge, with one main arch and two smaller flood arches, is still in use today, carrying cars across the river.

This impressive 60ft (18.2 metres) waterfall is situated in a lovely setting – a deep narrow gorge where rhododendrons grow. It is just a short walk from Dalegarth Station on the Ravenglass and Eskdale Railway.

Another view of Pelter Bridge just outside Rydal. Note the roads have not yet been paved in this scene, and are merely tracks of dirt.

Ruskin's Monument, Coniston Churchyard.

John Ruskin was a poet, artist and art critic who lived in Coniston until his death in 1900. He is buried in St Andrews churchyard in the village – his grave is marked by a green slate cross made in the local quarry.

Coniston Hall and Old Man   S.641

Coniston Water is the third largest lake in the Lake District and is well known for the peak The Old Man of Coniston that rises behind it. It can be seen here in this 1950s view of the edge of the lake, towering behind the caravan park.

67. CONISTON LAKE FROM BEACON CRAGS.

Looking down on Coniston Water and a landing pier from Beacon Crags, which ascend from the southern end of the lake, which stretches five miles in length to the village of Coniston at its northern end.

40345. CONISTON LAKE FROM LAKE BANK.

The tranquil view of Coniston Water seen here is a far cry from the excitement and tragedy experienced on the lake when Donald Campbell attempted to break the world speed record on water. He had already broken several records in the 1950s, and in 1967 was attempting to break it again when his craft, the Bluebird K7, flipped and crashed at high speed, killing Campbell.

The centre of Coniston village as seen in the 1930s, with no road traffic or people in sight. The Black Bull inn is on the right of the picture, with the bridge over Church Beck in the foreground. Rising in the distance is the peak of the Old Man of Coniston.

Aside from its Priory, Cartmel is a lovely village south of the Lakes. This view looking from the bridge which passes over the River Esk shows some of the traditional cottages within the village, as seen from outside the present-day Kings Arms pub.